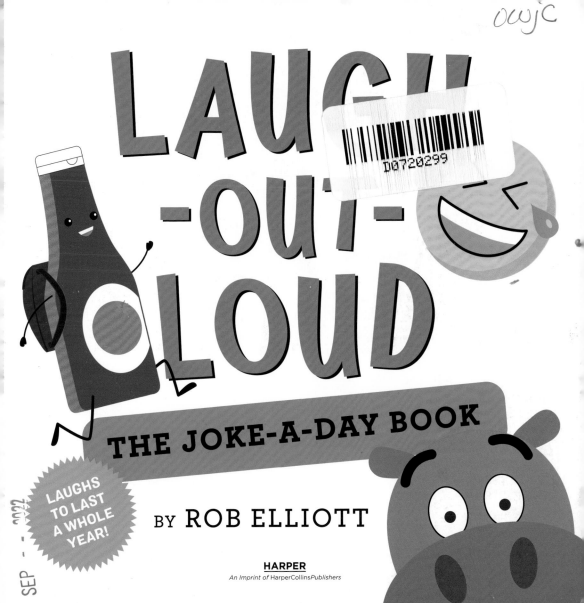

LAUGH-OUT-LOUD

THE JOKE-A-DAY BOOK

LAUGHS TO LAST A WHOLE YEAR!

BY ROB ELLIOTT

HARPER
An Imprint of HarperCollinsPublishers

Knock, knock.

Who's there?

Omelet.

Omelet who?

Omelet smarter than I look!

What do snowmen say when they play hide-and-seek?

I-cy you!

Knock, knock.

Who's there?

Spell.

Spell who?

W-H-O!

What do penguins use in science class?

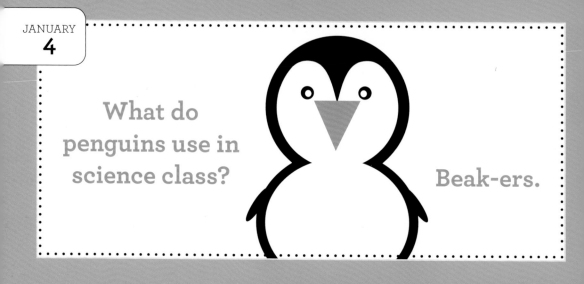

Beak-ers.

What do SNOWMEN like on their CUPCAKES?

FROSTING!

Why wouldn't the **skeleton go snowboarding** down the mountain?

He didn't have the guts.

Knock, knock.

Who's there?

Donut.

Donut who?

Donut worry. I'm sure you'll pass your test!

What do you get when you combine a **penguin** and a **jalapeño?**

A chilly pepper.

Knock, knock.

Who's there?

Jamaica.

Jamaica who?

Jamaica good grade on your report card?

JANUARY
10

JANUARY
11

KNOCK, KNOCK.

Who's there?

NEEDLE.

Needle who?

Needle little help getting your homework done?

KNOCK, KNOCK.
Who's there?

EARS.
Ears who?

Ears looking at you, kid!

What happens if you check out too many library books?

You'll overdue it!

Knock, knock.

Who's there?

Repeat.

Repeat who?

Who,
who,
who,
who,
who,
who,
who,
who . . .

What do you get when you mix a

DOG

with a

SNOWFLAKE?

FROSTBITE.

What did the snowplow driver say at the end of the season?

"It was nice snowing you."

Knock, knock.
Who's there?

Orange.
Orange who?

Orange you glad
we don't have
school tomorrow?

yay!

Why don't
hyenas get sick
in the winter?

Because
laughter is the
best medicine.

Knock, knock.

Who's there?

Polka.

Polka who?

Polka me one more time, and I'll tell the teacher!

Why was the **snowman so mean?**

Because he was coldhearted.

KNOCK, KNOCK.

Who's there?

I AM.

I am who?

YOU DON'T
KNOW
WHO YOU ARE?

Why won't
PENGUINS use
CELL PHONES?

Because they're
cold-fashioned.

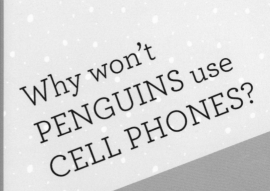

Knock, knock.
Who's there?
Ethan.
Ethan who?

Ethan teachers need a summer vacation!

Did you know lots of reindeer live in Alaska?

That's what we herd.

What do you call a COW that lives in an IGLOO?

An Eski-moo.

Knock, knock.
Who's there?

Feta.
Feta who?

I'm feta up with these knock-knock jokes!

What did the pirate say when he was freezing in the snow?

"Shiver me timbers!"

Knock, knock.
Who's there?
Leggo.
Leggo who?

Leggo of the
doorknob so
I can come in!

What's a
POLAR BEAR'S
favorite
CEREAL?

crackle! snap! POP!

Ice Krispies.

What kind of **bug loves** Valentine's Day?

A hopeless roman-tick.

POODLE:
Are you sure you want
to be my valentine?

GOLDEN RETRIEVER:

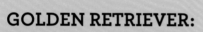
I'm paws-itive!

KNOCK, KNOCK.

Who's there?

RAISIN.

Raisin who?

You're the RAISIN
I'm so happy!

Knock, knock.
Who's there?

Owl.
Owl who?

Owl always love you!

Why did the girl eat her Valentine's candy before she went to bed?

She wanted sweet dreams.

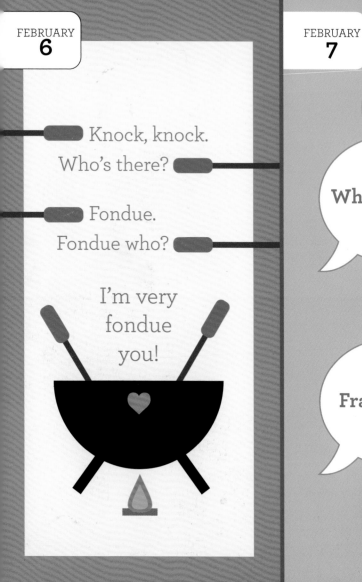

JACKSON:
Would you like a date on Valentine's Day?

JENNY:
I think I'd rather have some chocolate.

YUM
chocolate
ch

Knock, knock.
Who's there?

Wool.
Wool who?

**Wool you be
my valentine?**

KNOCK, KNOCK.

Who's there?

DONATE.

Donate who?

Donate make sense for you to be my valentine?

What do you sing when you're in love?

A valen-tune!

Did you hear that the **cow and bull broke up?**

Yes, they won't stop **beefing about it!**

Knock, knock.

Who's there?

Annie.

Annie who?

Annie valentines for me today?

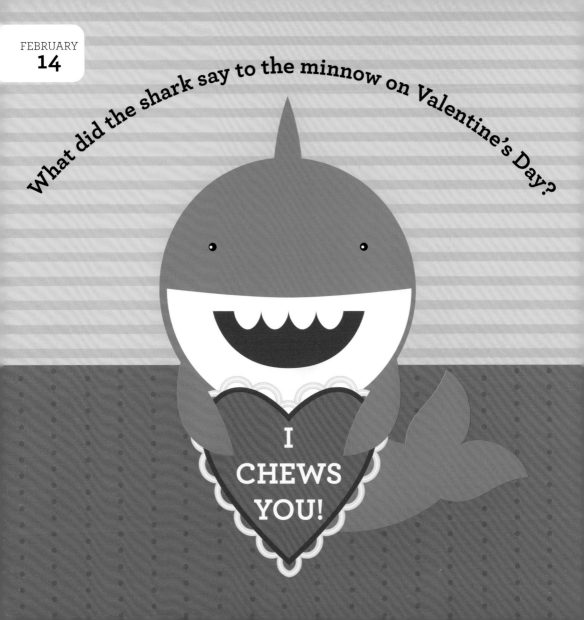

Knock, knock.
WHO'S THERE?

Pudding.
PUDDING WHO?

I'm **PUDDING** the final touches on my valentines.

Should we make dinner reservations for Valentine's Day?

No, let's just wing it!

Knock, knock.
Who's there?
Yoda.
Yoda who?

Yoda one
for me!

KNOCK, KNOCK.
Who's there?

POOCH.
Pooch who?

**Pooch your
arms around
me.**

FEBRUARY
19

FEBRUARY
20

What kind of shoes do you wear to surprise your valentine?

Sneakers.

What did the chef give his wife for Valentine's Day?

A hug and a quiche.

Why did the **bull go broke** after Valentine's Day?

$ He spent too much **MOOO-LA** $ on his date.

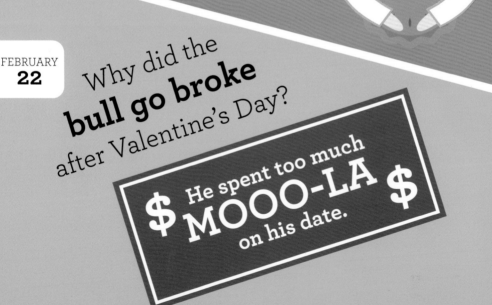

**FEBRUARY
25**

Knock, knock.
Who's there?

Bacon.
Bacon who?

I'm **bacon** you a cake for Valentine's Day!

**FEBRUARY
26**

Girl: Should we go sailing or canoeing on our date?

Boy:
It's either oar.

What did the computer do after it got home late from the Valentine's party?

It crashed.

KNOCK, KNOCK.
Who's there?
MELON.
Melon who?
YOU'RE ONE IN A MELON!

PONY: How was your Valentine's Day?

HORSE: Not good!

PONY: What happened?

HORSE: My date was a night-mare!

Knock, knock.
Who's there?

Atlas.
Atlas who?

**Atlas it's time for
the weekend!**

What is the smartest kind of bug?

the
BIG BOOK
of
ANT-SWERS

A brilli-ant.

Knock, knock.
Who's there?

Sharon.
Sharon who?

Sharon share alike with your classmates.

Knock, knock.
Who's there?

Minnow.
Minnow who?

Let minnow if you plan on letting me in!

How do PIGS RELAX on a spring day?

In a ham-mock.

What do pandas eat in the spring?

Straw-bearies.

Knock, knock.
Who's there?

Irish.
Irish who?

☑ Irish
☑ I could take the test over!
☑
☑

KNOCK, KNOCK.
Who's there?

ESPRESSO.
Espresso who?

Can I ESPRESSO
much I want to
come inside?

What do
leprechauns
eat for
breakfast?

Lucky
Charms.

Knock, knock.
Who's there?

H.
H who?

God bless you!

Why did the farmer take his cows to the gym?

**To build up
their moo-scles.**

MARCH
12

What's the
**HARDEST
STONE**
to throw?

A sham-rock!

MARCH
13

KNOCK, KNOCK.
Who's there?

IRAN.
Iran who?

Iran to catch the school bus, but I missed it!

Knock, knock.
Who's there?

Iguana.
Iguana who?

Iguana juice box in my lunch today.

What kind of **leprechaun** plays tricks on you?

A lepre-con.

Knock, knock. Who's there?

Walnut. Walnut who?

I walnut leave until you open the door!

Who can help me find a **four-leaf clover?**

A lepre-can!

What is a **GARDENER'S** favorite game?

TIC-TAC-GROW.

What's a leprechaun's favorite kind of music?

Shamrock!

Knock, knock.

Who's there?

Handsome.

Handsome who?

Handsome food to me—I'm starving!

Knock, knock.

Who's there?

Abby.

Abby who?

Abby stung me on the playground!

Why did the
POLAR BEAR
visit friends for
SPRING BREAK?

He had been feeling ice-olated.

Knock, knock.
WHO'S THERE?

Mustache.
MUSTACHE WHO?

I mustache the teacher a question about the test.

Where do writers go for spring break?

PENCIL-VANIA.

KNOCK, KNOCK.

Who's there?

RILEY.

Riley who?

I Riley hope I passed the test this time!

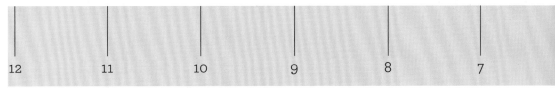

How can you see your garden in the dark?

Plant a lot of bulbs!

WHY CAN'T A NOSE BE TWELVE INCHES LONG?

| 12 | 11 | 10 | 9 | 8 | 7 |

Because then it would be a foot!

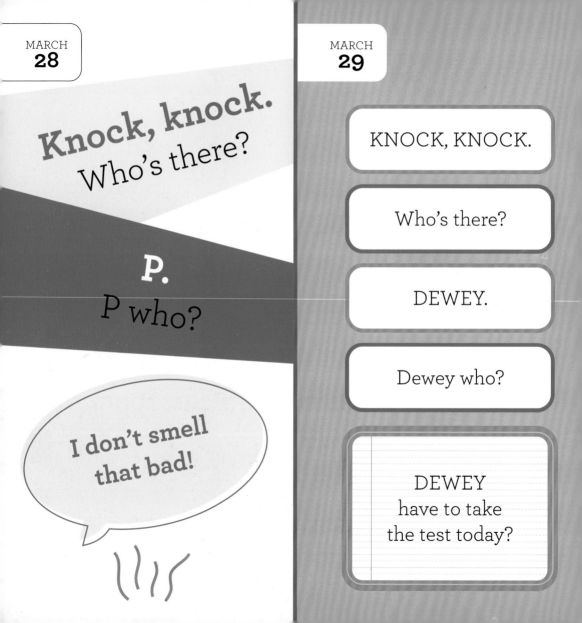

Why did the
CHICKEN
marry a
CATERPILLAR?

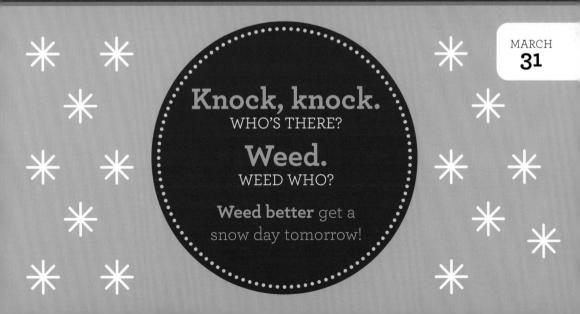

Because chicks dig worms.

Knock, knock.
WHO'S THERE?
Weed.
WEED WHO?

Weed better get a
snow day tomorrow!

What did the gardener do when all her plants wilted?

She
threw
in the
trowel.

Knock, knock.
Who's there?

Bunny.
Bunny who?

Some bunny ate
all my Easter candy!

When do the monkeys come out at the zoo?

In Ape-ril.

APRIL
4

Why did the
Easter Bunny
give away so
many **baskets?**

He was feeling
eggs-travagant.

APRIL
5

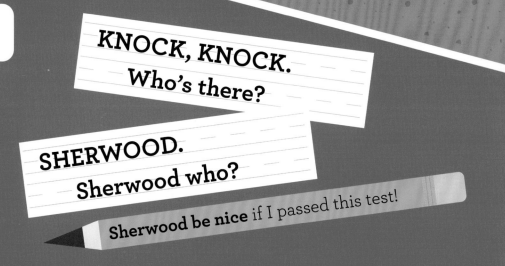

KNOCK, KNOCK.
Who's there?

SHERWOOD.
Sherwood who?

Sherwood be **nice** if I passed this test!

APRIL 6

How does Easter end?

With an R.

APRIL 7

Should we skip the chocolate bunnies for Easter this year?

No, that's a hare-brained idea!

Why did the farmer visit the chicken coop?

He wanted to hang out with his peeps!

Why did quarters start falling from the sky?

¢ 25 25 25 ¢ ¢ 25 25

There was **change** in the weather.

Knock, knock.
Who's there?
Olive.
Olive who?

Olive
springtime!

Customer:
Waiter, do you serve rabbit here?

Waiter:
Yes, we're happy to serve anyone.

MENU

Knock, knock.
Who's there?

Phillip.
Phillip who?

Phillip my Easter basket with candy, please!

Where do flowers go to school?

KINDER-GARDEN!

KNOCK, KNOCK.

Who's there?

WEIRDO.

Weirdo who?

WEIRDO YOU THINK they hid all the Easter eggs?

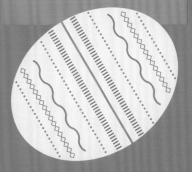

Why are **gardeners** never lonely?

They have a lot of buds.

Do you like your Easter basket?

It's eggs-actly what I was hoping for!

What do daylight saving time and a rabbit have in common?

They both spring forward.

Knock, knock.
Who's there?
Heidi.
Heidi who?

Heidi Easter eggs in the backyard.

Help, help, I'm dropping my Easter basket!

Get a grip!

Knock, knock.
Who's there?

Thumb.
Thumb who?

Thumbunny
loves you!

Knock, knock.
Who's there?

Robin.
Robin who?

Who's Robin
all my Easter
candy?

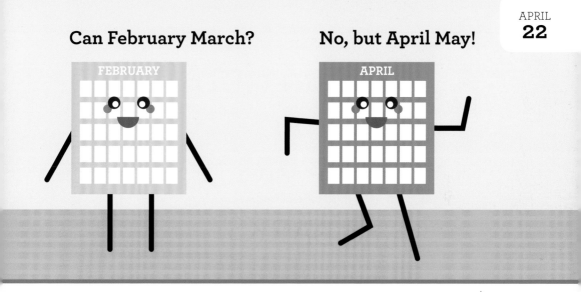

Can February March? No, but April May!

Where does the Easter Bunny stay on vacation?

At a
HARE
B and B.

APRIL
23

What kind of VEGETABLE

has FOUR LEGS

and BARKS?

A
COLLIE-FLOWER.

KNOCK, KNOCK.
Who's there?

KETCHUP.
Ketchup who?

Ketchup or
you'll be late
for school!

Why is the Easter Bunny so lucky?

He has four
rabbit's feet.

Why won't the **Easter Bunny** go down the chimney?

He doesn't want to catch the flue.

KNOCK, KNOCK.

Who's there?

STELLA.

Stella who?

STELLA 'nother Easter egg and I'm telling on you!

Farmer Bob:
How's your corn
growing this year?

Farmer Sue:
It's a-maize-ing!

What do you get
when you cross a
flower and a
merry-go-round?

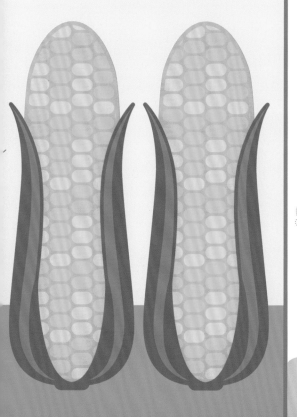

A dizzy
daisy.

KNOCK, KNOCK.

Who's there?

TURNIP.

Turnip who?

TURNIP
THE HEAT—
I'm freezing!

Knock, knock.
Who's there?

Hayden.
Hayden who?

**Hayden seek
is fun to play
at recess!**

What did the
ALIEN
say to the
gardener?

**Take me
to your
weeder.**

Knock, knock.

WHO'S THERE?

Elsie.

ELSIE WHO?

Elsie you after school.

It's raining cats and dogs!

April showers bring May flowers.

Yeah, but now there are poodles everywhere!

WHAT DO YOU GET WHEN YOU CROSS A **BIKE** AND A **FLOWER?**

Knock, knock.
Who's there?

Honeydew.
Honeydew who?

Honeydew you
know it's time
for school?

What are you
planting in
your garden
this year?

Beets me!

Knock, knock.
Who's there?

Leaf.
Leaf who?

Leaf your books
in your desk for
tomorrow.

WHY DID THE
BEE
HAVE TO GO TO THE
school nurse?

It was breaking
out in hives.

KNOCK, KNOCK.
Who's there?

HOUSE.
House who?

HOUSE
it going at
school today?

What do
sea turtles
like to study?

TODAY'S TIMES

Current events.

MAY
13

Do you like your new beard?

It's GROWING on me.

MAY
14

Knock, knock.
Who's there?

Toad.
Toad who?

I toad you to let me in!

Knock, knock.
Who's there?
Wayne.
Wayne who?

**Wayne will help
the flowers grow.**

What did **summer** say to **spring?**

Help, I'm going to **fall!**

MAY
17

Are you sure the atom lost an electron?

Yes, I'm positive!

MAY
18

Knock, knock.
Who's there?
Norma Lee.
Norma Lee who?

Norma Lee I like to play outside in the rain.

Why is England such a wet country?

It has a queen who's reigning.

How did Mary feel when her little lamb followed her to school?

Sheepish!

Your pig needs a bath.

HOGWASH!

KNOCK, KNOCK.
Who's there?
GLOVE.
Glove who?
Glove to hang out
with you in springtime.

Knock, knock.
Who's there?
Anita.
Anita who?

$ **Anita dollar**
for hot lunch! $

WHY ARE FLOWERS SO LAZY?

They're always in their beds.

KNOCK KNOCK.
Who's there?

ICE CREAM.
Ice cream who?

Ice cream for springtime!

MAY 26

What kind of snake comes out after it rains?

A rain-boa.

MAY 27

Knock, knock.
Who's there?

Abbott.
Abbott who?

Abbott time you finished all your homework!

WHAT DID THE EGG SAY TO THE CIRCUS CLOWN?

You crack me up!

Knock, knock.
Who's there?
Everest.
Everest who?

Everest in a hammock on a spring day?

Why are chickens so hard to get along with?

You're always walking on eggshells around them.

Knock, knock.

Who's there?

Juno.

Juno who?

Juno where to go for spring break?

Wish you were pier!

What do SHARKS like to play at RECESS?

SWALLOW THE LEADER!

Why did the horse keep falling down?

It wasn't very stable!

Knock, knock.

Who's there?

Oscar.

Oscar who?

Oscar SiLLY question, you get a SiLLY answer.

Knock, knock.
Who's there?

Gwen.
Gwen who?

Gwen will the flowers start blooming?

Why did the **jellyfish** always get **picked on** at school?

It didn't have any backbone.

KNOCK, KNOCK.
Who's there?

PIZZA.
Pizza who?

You want a pizza me?!

Knock, knock. Who's there?

Sid. Sid who?

Sid down and I'll tell you some jokes!

Ha! HA! Ha! Ha! Ha! HA! Ha! HA! Ha! HA! Ha! Ha! HA!

Why was the **toad** stressed out?

It was a
worry-wart.

Knock, knock.
WHO'S THERE?

Twister.
TWISTER WHO?

Twister key and unlock the door!

What should I wear when I visit Disneyland?

A Minnie skirt!

Knock, knock.
Who's there?

Moth.
Moth who?

Moth thumb got slammed in the door!

Why didn't
King Arthur
go to work?

He
took the
knight
off.

Knock, knock.
Who's there?
Aspen.
Aspen who?

Aspen
wanting to
tell more
knock-knock
jokes!

Why are
turtles
always throwing
parties?

**They like to
shell-ebrate!**

Knock, knock.

Who's there?

Token.

Token who?

I'm token to you.
Let me in!

KNOCK, KNOCK.
Who's there?

LLAMA.
Llama who?

Llama in!
It's cold
out here!

What happens when
your foot falls asleep?

It's coma-toes.

KNOCK, KNOCK.
Who's there?
WOODEN SHOE.
Wooden shoe who?

Wooden shoe like to go canoeing today?

Knock, knock.
Who's there?

Radio.
Radio who?

RADIO NOT, here I come!

How smart are you?

I'm so bright my mom calls me "sun"!

Knock, knock.
Who's there?

Disgusting.
Disgusting who?

Dis-gusting wind is blowing my papers all over.

What do you get when **paper towels** fall asleep?

Napkins!

Do you like how I ironed your shirt?

Yes, I'm im-pressed!

Why couldn't the pirate play cards?

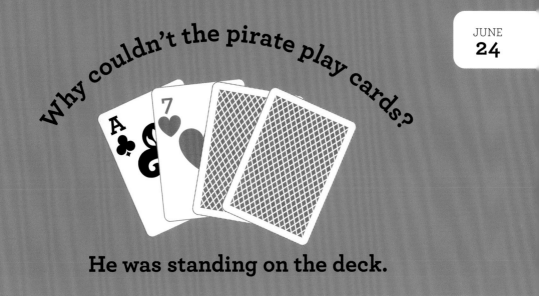

He was standing on the deck.

Knock, knock.
Who's there?

Macon.
Macon who?

I'm Macon some eggs and bacon. You want some?

What do you get
when it rains in
Paris?

French
puddles.

C'est
magnifique!

Ooh
La
La!

Knock, knock.
Who's there?

Shell.
Shell who?

Shell
be coming
around the
mountain when
she comes.

What is an artist's favorite kind of juice?

CRAYON-BERRY.

KNOCK, KNOCK.

WHO'S THERE?

HANK.

HANK WHO?

Hank you for answering the door!

What do
trees
put on their
salad?

BRANCH
DRESSING

Knock, knock.
Who's there?

Mason.
Mason who?

It's pretty
a-Mason
that I'm still
knocking.
Answer the door!

KNOCK, KNOCK.
Who's there?
EUROPE.
Europe who?

**Europe very early
this morning.**

**Why did the
fish go to jail?**

**Because it
was gill-ty.**

KNOCK, KNOCK.
Who's there?
WOOD.
Wood who?

WOOD YOU LIKE TO GO SWIMMING WITH ME?

I forgot to pack my bug spray!

That bites.

When do you quit doing laundry?

When you throw in the towel.

Knock, knock.
WHO'S THERE?

Noah.
NOAH WHO?

Noah great
place to go
camping?

What's a horse's favorite snack?

Hay-zelnuts.

Why don't melons run away together?

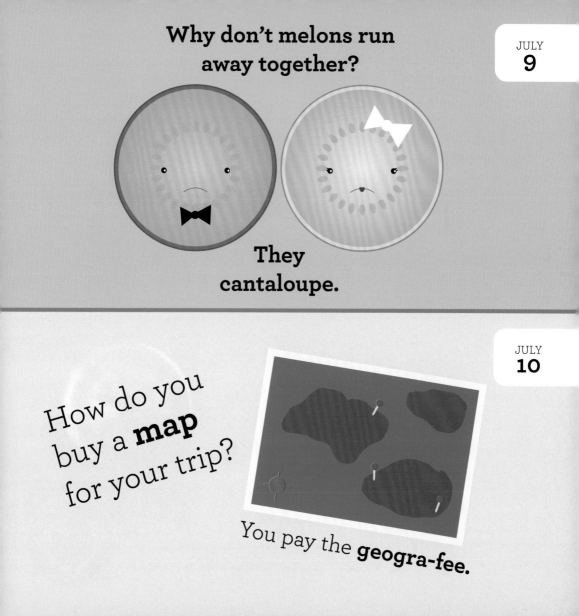

They cantaloupe.

How do you buy a **map** for your trip?

You pay the **geogra-fee.**

Knock, knock.
Who's there?

Peter.
Peter who?

Peter
boots on
so we can
go hiking!

How do you
get to your
accountant's
office?

In an income taxi.

Knock, knock.

Who's there?

Muffin.

Muffin who?

Muffin to do today—let's go have some fun!

What is an **elephant's** favorite dessert?

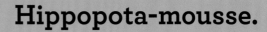

Hippopota-mousse.

How are your **scuba diving** lessons going?

Swimmingly!

Knock, knock.

Who's there?

Lena.

Lena who?

Lena little closer—I want to tell you a secret.

Knock, knock.
Who's there?
Dishes.
Dishes who?

**Dishes the police.
Come out with
your hands up!**

**How do
you see a**
Dalmatian
at night?

With a
spot-light.

How many antelope live in Africa?

Probably a gazelle-ion!

KNOCK, KNOCK.
Who's there?

PEEKA.
Peeka who?

No, it's peekaboo!

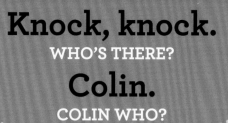

Why is the sun smarter than the moon?

The moon just isn't as bright.

Knock, knock.
WHO'S THERE?
Colin.
COLIN WHO?

Colin it a day! It's time to go.

Why do we have to stop at every filling station on the highway?

It isn't polite to pass gas.

How is **HAWAII** like your arms?

Hawaii has **tourists,** and your arms have **two wrists.**

Knock, knock.
Who's there?
Wendy.
Wendy who?

Wendy we go to the skate park?

When do you
need medicine
on a train?

When you have
loco-motion
sickness.

Knock, knock.
Who's there?
Pecan.
Pecan who?

**Pecan someone
your own size!**

What do you get
when you cross a
SURFBOARD
and a
HANDKERCHIEF?

A BOOGIE BOARD.

Where are there oranges, beaches, and Mickey Mouse?

In Flori-duh!

Knock, knock.
WHO'S THERE?

Howl.
HOWL WHO?

Howl I get in if you don't open the door?

Why did the whales watch the sunset?

They wanted a sea-nic view.

Knock, knock.

Who's there?

Hugo.

Hugo who?

Hugo first and I'll follow!

Knock, knock.

Who's there?

Sara.

Sara who?

Sara nother way around this lake?

What do motorcycle racers eat for lunch?

Fast food.

WHY DID THE KIDS TAKE THE ELEVATOR?

Because it's not polite to stair.

KNOCK, KNOCK.
Who's there?

CASINO.
Casino who?

CASINO REASON WHY YOU WON'T LET ME IN.

What's a
FROG'S
favorite
game?

Croak-ay.

Knock, knock.
WHO'S THERE?

Jester.
JESTER WHO?

Your **jester one** to open
the door for me!

Who gave
the mermaid a
new nose?

The plastic
sturgeon.

KNOCK, KNOCK.

Who's there?

DESIGN.

Design who?

Design says you're

OPEN

so let me in!

WHAT'S THE

craziest

animal

IN AFRICA?

A hyper-potamus!

What do you get when you cross a **trumpet** and a *watermelon*?

A TOOTY FRUITY!

Why was the butterfly embarrassed when it came to the dance?

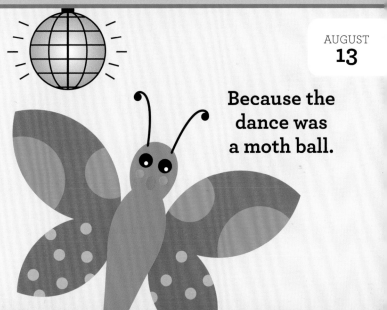

Because the dance was a moth ball.

When do boxers dress up in tuxedos?

When they want to look so-fist-icated.

KNOCK, KNOCK.
Who's there?

HOWELL.
Howell who?

Howell I get in if you don't open the door?

What happened when the gardener saw a monster?

She wet her plants.

My dog brought me a stick all the way from South America.

That sounds far-fetched.

Knock, knock.
Who's there?

Harry.
Harry who?

Harry up
so we can
get going!

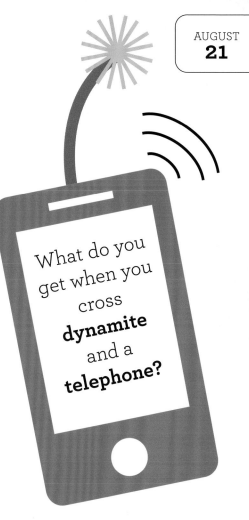

What do you get when you cross **dynamite** and a **telephone?**

A boomerang!

KNOCK, KNOCK.
Who's there?
S'MORE.
S'more who?

There s'more jokes where that came from!

KNOCK, KNOCK.
Who's there?

EMMA.
Emma who?

Emma 'bout to climb through the window!

What kind of cat
likes to swim?

A platy-puss.

KNOCK, KNOCK.
Who's there?

ISABELLA.
Isabella who?

Isabella going to
work or do I have to
keep knocking?

What kind of birds always get stuck in trees?

Vel-crows.

Knock, knock.

Who's there?

Ava.

Ava who?

Ava got a good feeling about this.

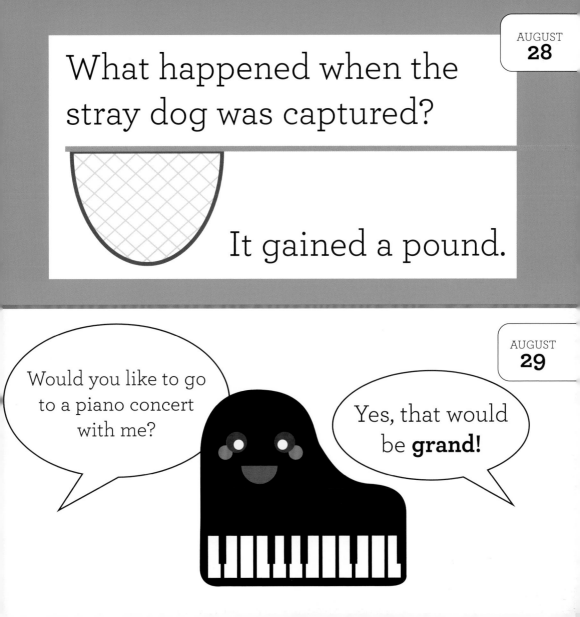

When do
scuba divers
sleep under
water?

**When they're
snore-kling.**

Knock, knock.
Who's there?
Ruth.
Ruth who?

**I have peanut
butter stuck
on the Ruth
of my mouth!**

KNOCK, KNOCK.
WHO'S THERE?

TWAIN.
TWAIN WHO?

Twain hard and you can join the soccer team.

When are all the books in the library the **same color?**

When they're all read.

I thought of a joke about sodium and hydrogen.

Would you like to share it with the class?

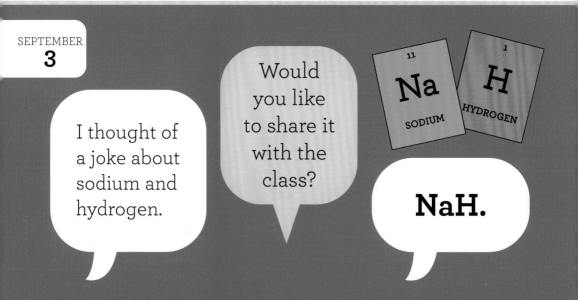

11

Na

SODIUM

1

H

HYDROGEN

NaH.

Where did the
sick peach
nap at the school
nurse's office?

**In an
apri-cot.**

Knock, knock.
WHO'S THERE?

Joe King.
JOE KING WHO?

Joe King
too much
will get you
sent to the
principal's
office!

SEPTEMBER
6

What can you tell me about Greece?

GREASE
FROM GREECE

It's slippery!

SEPTEMBER
7

Knock, knock.
Who's there?
Mushroom.
Mushroom who?

How mushroom do you have left in your backpack?

SEPTEMBER
8

Jill, why did you miss class yesterday?

I didn't *miss* it, but I was sick!

SEPTEMBER
9

Knock, knock.

Who's there?

Gopher.

Gopher who?

Gopher the best grade you can get!

Where did the rabbit go when he couldn't see the chalkboard?

To the hop-thalmologist.

KNOCK, KNOCK.
Who's there?

STOPWATCH.
Stopwatch who?

Stopwatch you're doing and listen to the teacher!

Why did the
student
wear a
shower cap
to school?

He didn't want to
get brainwashed.

Knock, knock.
Who's there?

Sweet tea.
Sweet tea who?

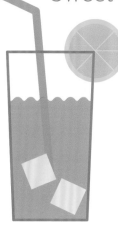

Be a **sweet tea**
and carry my
backpack.

Why do you have to keep an eye on your art teacher at all times?

BECAUSE THEY'RE CRAFTY.

Who can tell me the capital of Washington?

W.

Knock, knock.
Who's there?

Quiche.
Quiche who?

Quiche me quick
before I go!

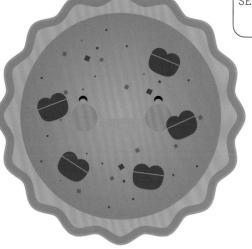

How much did
the wasp pay for its
school supplies?

Nothing.
It got free-bees.

SEPTEMBER
18

Why did the
baseball coach
go to the
bakery?

He needed a batter.

SEPTEMBER
19

How was school today?

There was a kidnapping in our class today.

Oh no! What happened?

The teacher woke him up and gave him detention.

KNOCK, KNOCK.
Who's there?
YAH.
Yah who?

What are you so excited about?

What can you
HEAR
but never
TOUCH
or **SEE?**

Your voice.

Knock, knock.
Who's there?

Lettuce.
Lettuce who?

Lettuce in and you'll find out!

Why did the kid's pants fall down in choir?

He was belting it out!

Why did you plant your math book in the ground?

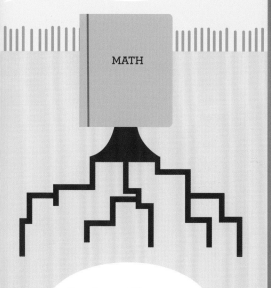

MATH

So it will grow square roots!

Knock, knock.
Who's there?
Sawyer.
Sawyer who?
Sawyer bus at the bus stop.

Can you give me an example of an interrogative sentence?

Do I have to?

Well done!

KNOCK, KNOCK.
Who's there?

TACO.
Taco who?

I could taco 'bout my family vacation all day.

What do dogs do when they're scared?

They flea! (flee)

Do you like your book about gravity?

Yes, I can't put it down!

KNOCK, KNOCK.

Who's there?

NANA.

Nana who?

NANA YOUR BUSINESS.

What happened when
Frankenstein
heard the joke?

He was in
stitches!

Knock, knock.

WHO'S THERE?

Itchy.

ITCHY WHO?

Bless you!
Do you need
a tissue?

Knock, knock.
Who's there?
Canopy.
Canopy who?
**Canopy outside when
we go camping?**

Did you finish your panda costume for Halloween?

Bearly!

Why did Dracula need glasses?

He was blind as a bat.

Knock, knock.
Who's there?
Granite.
Granite who?
Don't take me
for granite!

Who is the
best dancer
at the monsters'
ball?

The
boogieman.

What do you call a

ZOMBIE

elephant?

Gro-tusk!

Knock, knock.
Who's there?

Geyser.
Geyser
who?

**Geyser
just as good
at telling jokes
as girls.**

How was your day, son?

I got in trouble with the teacher for something I didn't do.

Oh no, what happened?

I didn't do my homework.

Knock, knock.
Who's there?
Window.
Window who?

Window I get to tell another joke?

Who's in charge of the tooth fairy?

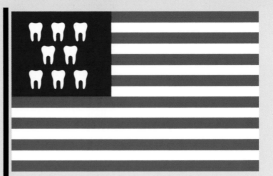

The presi-dentist.

Why do skeletons always laugh at your jokes?

They find everything humerus.

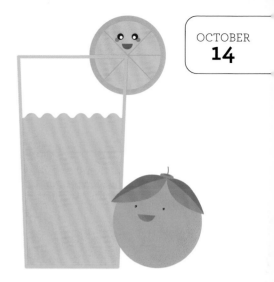

Knock, knock.
Who's there?
JUICY.
Juicy who?

Juicy any reason
I shouldn't tell another
knock-knock joke?

How did
Benjamin Franklin
feel when he discovered
electricity?

He was
shocked!

Why did the kids go to the haunted house?

It was eerie-sistible.

Knock, knock.

Who's there?

 Iowa.

Iowa who?

Iowa lot of lunch money in the cafeteria.

What do
you get if you
scare a tree?

Petrified wood!

Knock, knock.
Who's there?

Raymond.
Raymond who?

Raymond me to wear my helmet
when I'm biking.

Does the library have any newspapers or magazines?

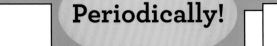

Periodically!

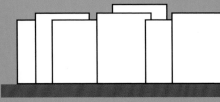

I finally found my watch.

It's about time!

HARRY:
My mom won't let me ride the Ferris wheel.

HENRY:
That's not fair!

What do **ghosts** wear to **climb** a mountain?

Hiking boo-ts!

Knock, knock.
Who's there?

Pasture.
Pasture who?

Pasture house on the way
to the park and thought I'd stop by.

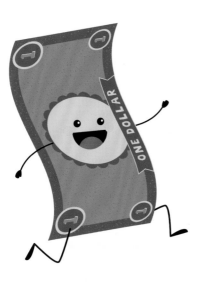

KNOCK, KNOCK.
Who's there?
MONEY.
Money who?

**Money is sore from
running all day.**

Why did you give away a fireplace for free?

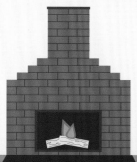

You must have a big hearth.

Knock, knock.
Who's there?
Alex.
Alex who?
Alex plain the joke later!

Where do scarecrows go for fun?

On field trips.

Knock, knock.
Who's there?
Odyssey.
Odyssey who?

Odyssey who's at
the door before
I answer it.

What kind of **MONSTER** tucks you in at night?

A mom-bie

**KNOCK,
KNOCK.**
Who's there?

CANDY.
Candy who?

Candy kids
come out
and play?

**Do you believe
gambling is good for
the economy?**

You bet!

KNOCK, KNOCK.

Who's there?

WELCOME.

Welcome who?

WELCOME WITH YOU WHEN YOU GO FOR A RIDE.

KNOCK, KNOCK.

Who's there?

SAFARI.

Safari who?

Safari like this funny joke book!

NOVEMBER
4

Is Alex disappointed that he caught a cold for the holidays?

He'll get over it.

NOVEMBER
5

Did you hear we're just having sandwiches for Thanksgiving dinner?

That's a bunch of baloney!

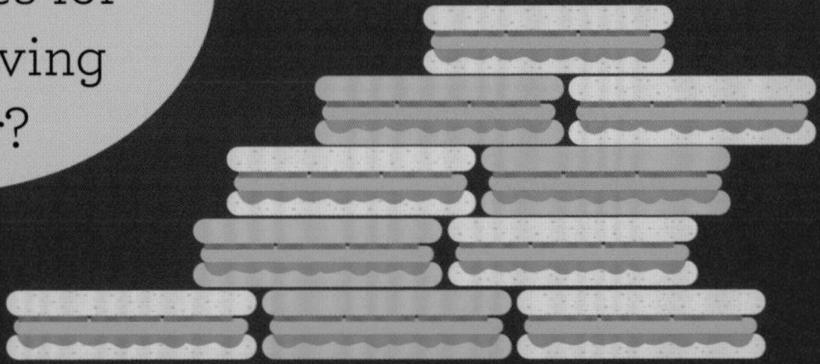

Why did the
PIG
always get
in trouble
in class?

Whoopie!

Because he
was such a
HAM!

Knock, knock.
Who's there?
Alaska.
Alaska who?

Alaska
student
and see if
he knows
the answer.

Knock, knock.

Who's there?

Judah.

Judah who?

Judah thought we'd go on vacation by now.

What SHOES did the BAKER wear while baking HOLIDAY bread?

HIS LOAFERS.

What did the **RABBIT** say to the frog?

Hoppy Holidays!

**Knock, knock.
Who's there?**

Alto.
Alto who?

Alto the boat to the lake.

How does a **grizzly** get through the **holidays?**

He'll grin and bear it.

Knock, knock.
Who's there?

Howdy.
Howdy who?

Howdy come up with this crazy joke?

What do you get
when you hang a
turkey from the
fireplace?

A stocking
stuffer.

Why can't you trust a pig with a secret?

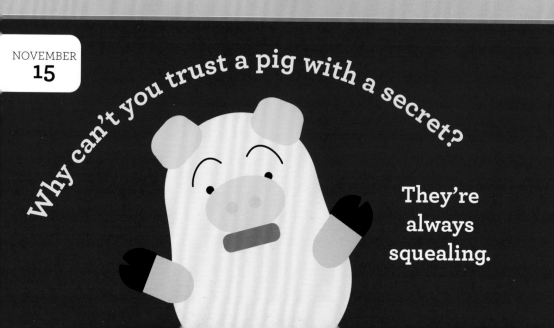

They're
always
squealing.

Knock, knock.
Who's there?

Firewood.
Firewood who?

A firewood warm things up in here!

Why won't SNOWMEN eat any CARROT CAKE?

They're afraid it has boogers in it.

KNOCK, KNOCK.
Who's there?

LION.
Lion who?

I'd be lion if I told
you I didn't love
the holidays.

What time is it
when a polar bear
sits in your chair?

I'm not sure.

It's time to get
a new chair.

OOPS!

Knock, knock.
    Who's there?
Cook.
    Cook who?

Clearly the holidays are
making you a little crazy!

Cook who? Cook who?
Cook who?
Cook who?
Cook who?
Cook who?

What's a turkey's favorite
Christmas dessert?

Blueberry gobbler.

Why was the dog
BARKING
at the fireplace?

It made him
 HOT
under the collar.

Knock, knock.
Who's there?

Duncan.
Duncan who?

Duncan cookies
in hot cocoa is
delicious!

What kind of
dinosaur
hibernates
for the winter?

A bronto-snore-us.

KNOCK, KNOCK.
Who's there?

COLD.
Cold who?

Cold you
come out
and build a
snowman
with me?

What do you call a
snowman's kids?

Chilled-ren.

What do you do if a polar bear is in your bed?

Find a hotel for the night!

Why do you sing
lullabies
to a snowbank?

So it can
drift
off to sleep.

How did the turkey get home for Christmas?

In a gravy boat.

What is a tree's favorite drink?

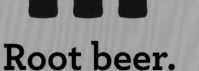

Root beer.

Why can't
PONIES
sing Christmas
CAROLS?

Because they're
a little horse.

Knock, knock.
Who's there?

Norway.
Norway who?

There is **Norway**
I'm kissing anybody
under the mistletoe!

DECEMBER 5

What do you have in

DECEMBER

that's not in any other month?

The letter D.

DECEMBER 6

I don't think we'll finish our Christmas story on time.

We'll have to book it!

Knock, knock.
Who's there?

Dubai.
Dubai who?

I'm off Dubai some Christmas presents for you!

KNOCK, KNOCK.
Who's there?

BUTTER.
Butter who?

You butter watch out.
You butter not cry.
You butter not pout I'm telling you why. . . .

Do you know how much Santa paid for his sleigh and reindeer?

Maybe a few bucks?

Nothing! It was on the house.

What is the **coldest** month of the year?

Decemb-rrrrr.

Did your goat eat my hat and mittens?

Yes, he scarfed them right down.

What do you get when you combine **Santa Claus** and **Sherlock Holmes?**

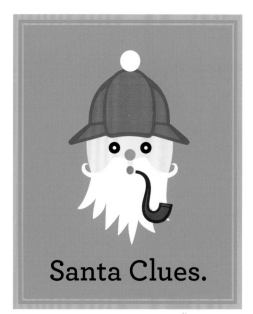

Santa Clues.

KNOCK, KNOCK.
Who's there?

TIBET.
Tibet who?

Go Tibet early
tonight, because
Santa is coming!

Did you
have fun at
the Christmas
party?

No, it was a
Feliz Navi-dud.

KNOCK, KNOCK.

Who's there?

YA.

Ya who?

WOW, ya really excited about Christmas!

I broke my candy cane in two places.

Then don't go to those places anymore!

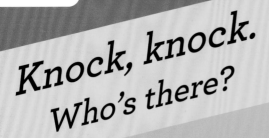

Knock, knock.
Who's there?

Avenue.
Avenue who?

Avenue started your Christmas shopping yet?

What kind of cookies make Santa laugh?

Snickerdoodles.

KNOCK, KNOCK.
Who's there?

SNOW.
Snow who?

I snow what Santa's bringing you for Christmas.

Did the cow like the present you got him?

No, he thought it was udderly ridiculous.

DECEMBER
21

Knock, knock.

Who's there?

Anna.

Anna who?

Anna partridge in a pear tree.

DECEMBER
22

What did the candy cane say to the ornament?

Hang in there.

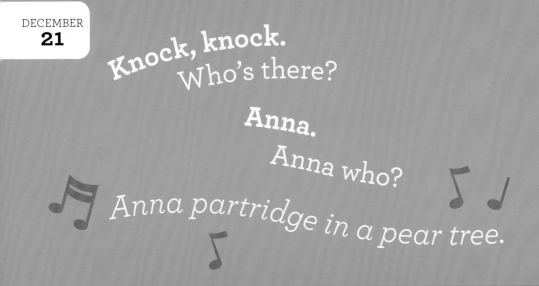

KNOCK, KNOCK.
Who's there?

ARTHUR.
Arthur who?

Arthur any more
Christmas presents
to open?

Why did you give me worms for Christmas?

TO: YOU
FROM: ME

Because they were dirt cheap!

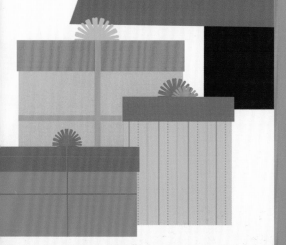

Was your mom surprised when she got a rug for Christmas?

She was floored!

What's the best music for decking the halls?

A-wreath-a Franklin!

KNOCK, KNOCK.
Who's there?

JUSTIN.
Justin who?

You're
Justin time
for Christmas
carols.

Knock, knock.
Who's there?

Oldest.
Oldest who?

Oldest Christmas shopping is giving me a headache!

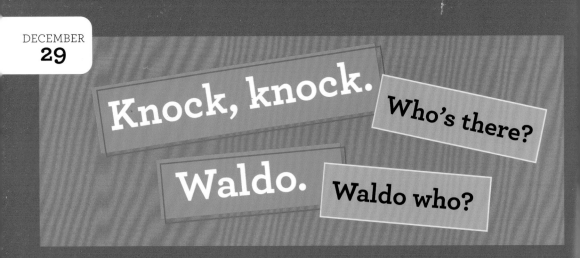

DECEMBER 29

Knock, knock.

Who's there?

Waldo.

Waldo who?

Waldo we do to celebrate New Year's Eve?

DECEMBER 30

KNOCK, KNOCK.

Who's there?

SNOW PLACE.

Snow place who?

There's snow place like home.

Knock, knock.
Who's there?

Water.
Water who?

Water you doing for New Year's Eve?

To my amazing wife, kids,
and the newest addition to our family, my grandson Reid.
You bring joy and laughter to my life 365 days a year.

Laugh-Out-Loud: The Joke-a-Day Book
Text copyright © 2022 by Robert E. Teigen
Illustrations copyright © 2022 by HarperCollins Publishers
Illustrations by Stacey Anderson
All rights reserved. Manufactured in Italy.

For information address HarperCollins Children's Books, a division of HarperCollins Publishers, 195 Broadway, New York, NY 10007.
www.harpercollinschildrens.com

Library of Congress Control Number: 2022932403
ISBN 978-0-06-308064-5

The artist used Adobe Illustrator to create the digital illustrations for this book.
Typography by Jessica Nordskog and Andrea Vandergrift, Production Management by Stonesong
22 23 24 25 26   RTLO   10 9 8 7 6 5 4 3 2 1
❖
First Edition